MANAGING THE FLEXIBLE WORKFORCE

MANAGING THE FLEXIBLE WORKFORCE

Richard Pettinger
Richard Pettinger Ltd.

The Busy Manager Series –
Best Practice Management Reports

Technical Communications (Publishing) Limited

ISBN 1 85953 071 0

© R. Pettinger, 1996

Technical Communications (Publishing) Ltd.
PO Box 6
Hitchin
Hertfordshire SG5 2DB
England

Telephone/Fax: (01462) 437075

Printed in England

Contents

Preface

Everywhere in the world there is a revolution going on, a transformation of business and of the services needed and wanted by people. There is a realization that, however organizational activities were organized and conducted in the past, new ways and better methods are essential for the future. Above all, this means a better understanding of the nature of work and recognition that all organizations need to get the most from their resources – including their people. Work methods and working patterns need to be devised which fit into all of this.

Ever greater strains and demands are placed on finite and diminishing resources. These have to be arranged, planned, ordered and organized to ensure that they are used to greatest possible advantage. There is therefore a constant drive for improvement in efficiency and effectiveness in work activities. Structured, orderly, hierarchical types of organization are increasingly seen as a constraint on successful activities.

The drive is towards flexibility, dynamism, responsiveness – qualities which lead to increased levels of customer service. This has been brought about by changing levels of customer expectations, much of which is the result of improvements in product quality and levels of service occasioned by technological advances and the successful performance of the industries of the Far East. In terms of public services, resource pressures are a real problem and this is certain to continue for the foreseeable future.

Flexible approaches to work are designed to address these issues. At their heart lies the need of organizations to maintain long-term existence, success, profitability and effectiveness in a rapidly changing and turbulent world. The best way to do this is to ensure that the people concerned – the staff – have the necessary skills, qualities, attitudes and approaches to work. From an organization's point of view, this means attention to the demands of its own particular customers and creating work methods and patterns that are suitable.

The purpose of this report is to cover the main issues that have to be faced. Chapter 1 is a discussion of the managerial approach to flexible working. Chapter 2 is a description and analysis of flexible work patterns and the advantages and disadvantages of using particular forms of employment. Chapter 3 covers the contractual arrangements that have to be faced. Chapter 4 discusses in detail the different managerial aspects of arranging, planning, co-ordinating and controlling flexible working; management training, style and attitudes; motivation and attitude formation; training and development; problem-solving; and the other aspects of management which

must be present if successful flexible working is to be carried out. Chapter 5 is a short summary and conclusion.

Jargon has been avoided as far as possible. Where specific technical terms are used, these are explained. There is also a glossary at the end of the report.

About the author

The author, Richard Pettinger, is an expert in human resource and industrial relations management. He has lectured, trained, consulted and advised extensively on all aspects of staff management and organizational behaviour.

He has advised on the implementation of flexible and alternative working methods in both the public and private sector. He has advised and consulted on the employment law aspects of flexible working. He has advised, consulted and prepared procedures and standards of best practice and performance for private companies, public bodies, local authorities, national health trusts and not-for-profit organizations.

Richard Pettinger is the author of *Introduction to Management*, published by Macmillan in 1994, and *Preparing and Handling Industrial Tribunal Cases*, published by Technical Communications (Publishing) Limited in 1995. He has two other books, *Introduction to Corporate Strategy* and *Introduction to Organizational Behaviour*, published by Macmillan in 1996.

The author is especially interested in working with all organizations wishing to raise their standards and understanding of staff management and industrial relations. He takes the view that excellent practice in these areas is a critical contribution to effective and profitable performance. He also consults and advises on all aspects of employment law and practice.

For further information, please contact:

Richard Pettinger
7 Victoria Place
Saltwood
Hythe
Kent CT21 4PY

Tel/Fax: (01303) 262388

Acknowledgement

I am very grateful for the advice and guidance of Kelvin Cheatle, Rebecca Frith and Glyn Jones in the preparation of this report.

Richard Pettinger
February 1996

1   Introduction

Flexible working is the term used to describe the creation of work patterns and arrangements based on the need to maximize and optimize organizational output, customer satisfaction and staff expertise and effectiveness. It has come about as the result of the expansion of globalization of competition and choice, increased pressures on all resources, enhanced customer demands and expectations, and changes in patterns of consumption.

Flexible workforces are created to maximize and optimize the use of capital, premises, technology and equipment, to produce high quality products and services that are available to customers where and when required.

Flexible working is not new. Energy, telecommunications, emergency services, health care, transport, and travel and leisure services have always operated around the clock. Personal selling – of insurance, building products, double glazing – has always taken place at times suitable to customers, especially evenings and weekends. Since the middle of the 1980s much of this has been extended into retail, banking and some office services.

Flexible work and extended working hours have therefore been around for a long time. The purpose here is to consider the potential, the opportunities and also the pitfalls afforded by flexible working in order to ensure that organizations that follow this path gain the best results possible, identify the best approaches and avoid the main problems.

Flexible Workforce

The flexible workforce is a combination of:

-     patterns of work, based on hours, expertise, the needs and demands of customers and clients, the capability and capacity of technology, location and specific aspects of particular activities;

-     attitudes and values, especially responsibility, dynamism, individual and collective responsiveness, commitments to service and satisfaction, and positive approaches to solving problems;

-     a commitment to training and development, enhancing the value brought by all members of staff to the organization;

- individual and collective commitment to improve all aspects of work, procedures, practices and response times, as well as products and services;

- organizational commitment to flexibility and to each of the above points, and a commitment to invest in and support everything that is necessary to achieve this.

Flexibility

Flexibility is a corporate attitude, and the flexible workforce is the product of this corporate attitude.

The reasons for having a flexible workforce are:

- to produce better quality, more effective work;

- to develop the reservoir of talent and potential that exists in all workforces, and which traditionally has remained constricted by procedures and hierarchies or otherwise largely untapped;

- to serve customers and clients at times suitable to them. This is especially true of retail and other service activities, following the decision of supermarkets, agencies, restaurants and other shops to open for longer hours, and following the Sunday Trading Act 1992 which further extended their scope for opening;

- to make full use of talented persons who (for a variety of reasons) are unable to work regular or traditional patterns or hours, and to harmonize their capabilities with the demands of customers and the requirements of organizations.

Key Qualities

For effective flexible work to take place, the following must be present.

- **Staff commitment:** to the organization, its customers, clients, products and services; to the quality of whatever is offered; to customer satisfaction and contentment.

- **Organizational commitment:** to its staff, its products, its services, its customers and its clients; to improvement in all areas and activities, including the quality of management and administration; to continuous training and development to improve the capabilities and expertise of the workforce.

2

- **Dynamism and responsiveness:** rather than passiveness and dependency on procedures and bureaucracy.

- **Empathy:** with customers and clients; with managements and supervision; with peers, superiors and subordinates; with suppliers and distributors; with governors, shareholders and backers.

- **Identity:** between the organization and its staff; between the organization and its customers and clients; within immediate work teams; with its wider environment and community; and with others with whom the individual comes into contact.

This is underpinned by the creation and development of positive attitudes and values in all areas. The responsibility for this rests entirely with the organization. None of this can take place without organizational commitment. Flexibility and capability in skills, knowledge, attitude, behaviour and expertise all feed off each other, leading to greater all-round understanding, capability and confidence, and to the required levels of commitment.

Expectations

Flexible attitudes and approaches to work raise the expectations of everyone. Shareholders, governors and directors of organizations expect increased levels of efficiency, effectiveness, profitability, all-round performance and all that these entail – improved morale, increased sales and levels of service, increased customer satisfaction, reduced levels of complaints, better and fuller use of technology and equipment, and higher returns on investment.

Staff expect an increased job interest and satisfaction, work variety, opportunities for training, development and advancement, and higher pay and reward levels. They anticipate greater feelings of identity. By virtue of being multi-skilled, they expect greater job and employment security. They expect to be redeployed rather than made redundant when one set of activities comes to an end. They expect to be consulted on work methods and patterns, to form levels of performance, to know what is going well and why, and what could be improved.

Customers expect product quality and service levels to be maintained and improved. They expect to be valued. They anticipate a long and beneficial relationship. Because of the increases in competition and choice, they are entitled to expect these high levels of quality and service, and organizations must anticipate that customers will look elsewhere for satisfaction if this is not forthcoming or if levels and quality fall.

3

Pitfalls

There are potential problems in raising the expectations of everyone concerned and then not being able to meet them. Successful flexible working therefore arises as the result of a strategic decision that this is the best way forward for the particular organization, department or division. It consists of:

- a long-term commitment to creating the necessary environment and conditions, supported and resourced by top management;

- a long-term view of the results desired. These do not happen overnight and the benefits may not be apparent for months or even years;

- a long-term commitment to creating the required skills, knowledge, attitudes, behaviour and expertise. This includes training programmes; job rotation; enlargement and enrichment; opportunities for project work and secondments; the development of potential for the future; the drawing out of talents and capabilities of everyone, identifying their strengths and weaknesses and maximizing the use of strengths;

- a commitment to organizational performance based on the long-term view rather than the pursuit of instant or short-term results. Again, this requires continuous and substantial investment in training and development, technology, attention to work methods, procedures and practices, an attitude of continuous improvement of everything in and around the workplace – all of which is conducted in the pursuit of customer satisfaction;

- a commitment to supporting staff, supervisors and managers in their decisions and activities.

Conclusion

Flexible working is a form of organizational investment, the purpose of which is getting the best out of existing and finite resources, especially the workforce. It is only successful and effective if organizations and their top managers:

- take a long-term view – the creation of a flexible workforce requires time and resources, training and development, attention to work division and job descriptions, and attention to pay and rewards;

- reappraise and realign the duties and priorities of their middle managers and supervisors towards maximizing and optimizing staff performance and customer satisfaction, and away from short-term results and the operation of procedures and systems;

- streamline and simplify administrative procedures and systems in order to concentrate on primary performance, attitudes and behaviour and resolving (rather than institutionalizing) problems;

- realign their own priorities, objectives and targets in support of this.

Flexible working is not cheap. Some cost savings may be possible in some circumstances. For example, corporate accommodation costs can often be cut where people are employed in working from home. This may, in some circumstances, be extended to the removal of administrative activities and some forms of supervision.

Above all, flexible working requires long-term commitment. It stems from organizational policy and strategy. Only when that is clear can attention usefully and effectively be paid to:

- hours and patterns of work;

- contractual arrangements and implications;

- managing the flexible workforce.

2 Hours and patterns of work

Introduction

Flexible working has first to be seen in its broadest context:

- Careers and occupations that last 40 years based on a 40-hour working week for 48 weeks of the year are no longer viable. Everyone (whatever their expertise or preference) must expect to experience great changes in occupation and in the ways in which things are done, as well as the obsolescence of some occupations and the creation of new ones.

- Earnings levels no longer rise steadily, nor are they the product of a combination of loyalty, promotion and enhanced expertise. People tend to expect enhanced rewards today, rather than the promise of enhanced rewards tomorrow.

- Organizations increasingly structure their workforce according to the peaks and troughs of the workload. This in turn means contracting out some specialist activities to specialist organizations, rather than retaining expensive expertise in-house, especially when it is only occasionally required, and creating networks that can be called upon at short notice to handle problems or cater for sudden upturns in activity.

- The use of part-time workers and intermittent patterns of employment is being extended to cope with the peaks and troughs of business demand.

- The range of activities covered by alternative patterns of employment, especially homeworking and subcontracting, is being extended.

- The nature of the organization's activities must be considered and the particular pressures and constraints that are present – production and operational pressures, any constraints placed by technology, the demands of customers and the nature of their relationship with the organization.

- There is a blurring of the distinction between full-time and part-time patterns of employment. In the UK there is now very little difference in basic employment rights between full-time and part-

time staff, and it is normally best practice to treat them exactly the same (see also Chapter 3 below).

This is the context in which consideration of different patterns of employment and hours of work takes place. The overall drive is to synchronize employee working hours with operational demands. This has the purpose of having people present when they are needed, and not present when they are not needed. It reduces costs, improves the effectiveness of the human resource and ultimately improves organizational performance.

Work Content

Whatever the hours worked, or nature of the job to be done, the following characteristics need to be satisfied:

- people should have some degree of autonomy over the way tasks are to be achieved, and should have a certain amount of responsibility for their own work, for the resources that they use and for the way in which they structure and organize their working day;

- variety and autonomy should be present;

- repetitive tasks should be kept to a minimum;

- people should receive regular feedback on their performance, and this should be carried out face-to-face in the course of normal supervision;

- the place of the job in the wider scheme of things should be clearly understood;

- social contact should be available wherever practicable;

- learning, training and development opportunities should be inbuilt into work patterns;

- people need to know what is expected of them in terms of performance, attitude, behaviour and demeanour;

- people should be treated fairly and evenly at all times;

- work should have distinctive measures of success and failure, and people should know and understand the means by which success and failure are evaluated.

From the employee's point of view, therefore, the hours should be long enough and regular enough to enable a sufficient amount of work to be carried out to give feelings of satisfaction and achievement. The longer and more regular the hours, the quicker a real identity and commitment is generated. Where hours are short and intermittent, there is a pressure on managers and supervisors to take additional steps to build this identity and commitment quickly.

From the employer's point of view, the issue is the ability to integrate this with the frequency, regularity and length of work period that the employee is present and the output that is required, feasible or achievable. People on different hours and patterns of work have to be integrated with one another so that an effective working environment and relationship is created. The greater the ability to do this, the greater the reduction in the use and administration of procedures and problem-solving, thus freeing up time and resources for productive and profitable activities.

Whatever the nature or patterns of work, everyone works better in a clean, comfortable and wholesome environment. This does not mean luxury. Moreover, there are work pressures and constraints to be considered – especially where work is to be carried out in extremes of heat or cold, wet or dry, or in dangerous conditions. Within this context, it should normally be possible to provide everyone with: basic standards of comfort and cleanliness; rest, refreshment and meal-time arrangements; car parking or transport to and from the workplace; and adequate standards of warmth and comfort. Making these available to everyone reinforces the value, respect and esteem in which everyone is held, regardless of their pattern of work or length of working hours.

Note

It is true that in exceptional cases a bad working environment leads to a Dunkirk spirit among the staff. It is much more usual, however, for this to remain a point of contention and to become a real problem when other things go wrong. It is especially true for those who make only infrequent visits to the organization (for example, part-timers, field sales staff, homeworkers) – no one wants to go to a tatty, dirty or unkempt environment. People will tend to stay away as much as they possibly can and this reinforces, rather than breaks down, the barriers between them and their organization.

Hours of Work

The main patterns are as follows.

- **Annual hours:** where the number of hours of work required each

year of the employee is established and patterns of work agreed between the individual and the organization. In the UK the normal upper figure on this is 2,000 hours (which represents an equivalent of 40 hours per week for 50 weeks of the year).

- **Compressed working:** where 'full-time' hours are worked, but compressed into fewer working days – for example, instead of working eight hours a day for five days, people work ten hours per day for four days or even 12–15 hours per day for three days.

- **Term-time working:** in which those with responsibilities for school-age children are either given extensive unpaid leave, or else required to take their annual leave during the school holidays.

- **Continental shifts:** whereby people follow patterns of work such as four days on and two days off, or three days on and two days off so that the whole week is covered in a fair manner.

- **Hours to suit:** where the demands of the work are reconciled with the work time preferences of the employees.

- **Twilight shifts:** where work is offered between 5.30 pm and 10.30 pm to people (often married women, students and those of school age) enabling them to fit work around their other commitments.

- **Flexitime:** based on:

  - core periods, when attendance is compulsory, either for a given period every day, or for a given period on certain days;

  - optional time, which is attendance at other than core times, enabling employees to choose the time suitable to themselves when they are most productive and again to reconcile this with their other demands and commitments.

- **Job sharing:** where a single position is shared out between two or more persons. Job sharing works best when the post is shared between two persons. For reasons of administration and control, it is both unusual and impractical to share one post between more than three persons.

Notes

1.	**Long hours**
	On the face of it, having one member of staff working up to 60 hours per week and possibly taking work home in the evenings or

on their days off (or failing to take all their leave entitlement) is attractive, because a large return is being made on one salary. If there really is 60 hours' worth of high quality work to be done each week, this can only be sustained by one person in the very short term. Over longer periods, the quality of work, personal health and personal life all suffer.

There is a culture among managerial, professional and white-collar staff in the UK of the work-based lifestyle. This consists of putting in long hours to demonstrate commitment, loyalty and dedication. In many cases a proportion of social life becomes centred around work. Long hours are invariably necessary once in a while. If they are continually necessary, it is either because the job is too big for one person, or because the job holder is not capable of doing it.

This applies to other occupations. Employees, often quite willingly, carry out overtime or work additional periods during their time off. The end result again is stress and burnout. Moreover, the employee becomes disappointed, frustrated and angry when the overtime and extra shifts come to an end as their standard of living then suffers.

2. **Short hours**
    If hours are too short and intermittent, the employee has no opportunity to build up any true working relationship with colleagues, managers and supervisors or the organization. The result again is frustration and disappointment. This occurs even if for some reason employees have chosen their hours of work. Where short periods of work are required, where part-time is the normal employment pattern, hours should still be long and regular enough to build up a mutual identity and positive beneficial relationship.

3. Hours to suit should **only** be offered on the employee's terms alone, where the work permits this, or where there is otherwise no possibility of filling the vacancy.

4. Flexitime is attractive and popular with people, because it normally allows them to build up additional leave entitlement through the amount of hours that they work during the optional period. It is most commonly found in white-collar and service sectors, and is increasingly being extended to production and sales functions.

5. Problems with job sharing arise when, for some reason, it becomes impossible for the job sharers to continue to work together.

It may also be necessary to consider variations in work pressures – for example, where the job share splits the working week into mornings and afternoons, and where it is more stressful in the mornings, or where the working week is divided at Wednesday lunchtime and the work is more pressurized on Thursday and Friday than Monday and Tuesday.

6.   If additional hours are required, these should first be offered to existing staff. This is especially important where people are on patterns of low or infrequent attendance as it gives the opportunity to develop the total working relationship. This also reduces the need for unnecessary recruitment, selection, induction and job training, and the administrative burden that these create.

7.   Those on distinctive patterns of employment – for example, Saturday and Sunday crews in retail, permanent night shifts – need the same positive identity and commitment to be generated as everyone else. Otherwise, these groups may become isolated and this tends to lead to unofficial work regulation and canteen cultures.

Whatever the hours agreed, the main issues are:

• to get the best possible work out of the member of staff;

• to gain a proper professional and committed working relationship;

• to give the member of staff the opportunity to earn a fair living;

• to build a positive and mutually productive continuing relationship.

Other Patterns of Work

Enrichment

Job and work enrichment has the purpose of making all work as satisfying and fulfilling as possible. It applies to any form of work that becomes mundane, repetitive or routine, all of which tend to lead to disaffection and boredom – and therefore loss of performance. It takes the following forms.

• **Rotation:** in which the employee is changed or rotated through a variety of tasks, activities and workstations. This should occur regularly enough to generate interest, but not so regularly as to fragment the work being carried out.

- **Enlargement:** in which the employee is given additional tasks and (increasingly) responsibilities attached to the main duties. Additional tasks often include quality control, customer liaison and dealing with problems and queries.

- **Consultation:** in order to get the employee's views on the best way of carrying out the work, on new work and workstation design, on the choice of new equipment, on problems with existing equipment.

- **Training and development:** for current activities, for the future, to identify potential and aptitudes, to pursue personal choices and preferences.

- **Project work:** based on a combination of organizational requirements and personal drives. Much of this often stems from suggestion schemes and membership of work improvement groups and quality circles. Some of this may also arise from secondments and from the continuous need for fresh approaches to problems.

Enrichment builds on and reinforces positive attitudes and commitment. It strengthens the mutual identity and interest of employee and employer. It identifies personal potential and aptitudes, and enlarges the fund of talent and expertise available.

Empowerment

Empowerment is a form of job enrichment which involves employees in any or all of the following:

- taking on additional responsibility for administration, customer satisfaction, record-keeping, cashing up (for example, in restaurants and checkout work);

- taking on extra duties such as bank and retail cash desk and checkout staff taking on sales and customer service functions;

- being allowed to use initiative in acting in the organization's best interests in its dealings with its customers;

- setting up work improvement groups, quality improvement groups or quality circles which are given broad remits in which to work and are allowed initiative and responsibility to carry out their tasks;

- setting up suggestion schemes, especially those which give employees scope, and sometimes a budget, to put their proposals into practice and which reward them for extra profits made or reductions in costs.

Apart from tackling specific problems and issues, these activities contribute to employee and organizational development and reinforce commitment to product quality and customer service.

Homeworking

Homeworking is attractive all round. For the employer, there is no need to provide expensive production, operational or office space as that is the employee's home. For the employee, there is no need to travel to work. Homeworking is well established in various sectors – for example computer software, fashion and clothing sales, journalism, financial services, cosmetics. Its potential is limited only by the approach and attitude of organizations and the strong demands of large sectors of the population that they physically separate their working and non-working lives. There is great potential for administration, financial management, purchasing and supply to be carried out by people working at workstations established in their own homes – and potential therefore for organizations to curtail their requirements for premises.

Notes

1.   Homeworking employees are provided with all the facilities and equipment that they would have if they were working on the employer's premises. For white-collar staff this includes phone, computer, fax, stationery and access to copying, mail and postage facilities. For those engaged in production activities, this includes any tools of the trade, access to supplies and means of delivery. For those engaged in sales, this is likely to include a car as well as other office equipment.

2.   Payment for homeworking normally covers the use of any domestic equipment for work purposes (for example, telephone, computer, fax). It also normally includes paying an allowance in return for the member of staff using a part of their home as a workplace.

3.   Homeworkers can feel isolated; this is often because they *are* isolated, cut off from the mainstream of their organization. Homeworking requires the establishment of effective channels of communication. Regular face-to-face meetings, reviews of performance and the opportunity to discuss progress are essential and must form part of the way of working.

4.   People must be prepared to cope with the lack of regular contact, and the loss of social interaction and regular attendance at a designated place of work.

5.   Homeworking must be fair to everyone concerned. Those who are not offered the chance of homeworking feel let down. Those who are offered the chance of homeworking often feel that they are being marginalized and that their opportunities for promotion and variation are limited.

Fixed-Term Contracts

This is where people are taken on for a specific period of time to do a particular job, where there is a requirement for absence cover (e.g. maternity) or where people are taken on for the duration of a project however long that lasts.

The boundaries are clearly stated in advance so that it is known to both employee and employer when the work is to finish.

A form of fixed-term contract is also often used for research jobs and to pursue ideas to see if they have potential. Employers normally place a deadline by which likely results should at least become apparent.

Piecework and 'Job and Finish'

This is where the employee is paid per item. Most commonly used in industrial and production work, it is less popular now than in the past because the volume of work possible is governed by production technology and because it tended to concentrate on volume rather than quality.

Fee Paying Work

This is for employees who carry out work above and beyond the call of duty (one-off payments or honoraria).

Autonomous Work Groups

This is where the group has a set amount of work to carry out and how this is to be done is agreed by group members and its manager.

Autonomous Work Units

This is where the unit is a distinctive feature of a larger organization. It works in line with organizational policies and aims, and its performance is affected by its location.

Unit managers are responsible for getting the best out of the unit in the prevailing local conditions. They are given resources and support from the centre, and autonomy and authority to act independently within these constraints.

Seasonal Work

These patterns are used in order to cope with seasonal pressures (e.g. Christmas, summer).

On-call

This is where individuals and groups do not work regularly for the organization, but where they may be called in at short notice to cover for sudden upturns in demand or to handle crises. Some on-call schemes pay a regular retainer; others include this in the form of increased payments when the work is actually carried out.

Use of Subcontractors, Agencies and Specialists

Subcontractors

Subcontractors are used to avoid extensive and expensive activities, functions, systems and procedures in which the organization has no particular expertise. Organizations pay fees to individuals and companies to carry out these activities. This form of activity is found extensively in the building and construction sectors. Many organizations now use it for catering, security, cleaning and car leasing services. The subcontracting approach is bounded only by the imagination of organizations. It is possible to subcontract personnel and financial services, purchasing and supply, transport and distribution. In some sectors (e.g. telecommunications) much more mainstream and specialized work is also contracted out to satellite, subsidiary or 'networked' organizations.

Agencies and Specialists

Agencies and specialists are used to enhance particular aspects of organization performance. They are not a substitute for regular in-house expertise.

- Staff and employment agencies are used to fill short-term gaps (e.g. sickness cover). Agency staff should never constitute the regular workforce.

- Executive search agencies and headhunters are used where they have specialist knowledge of particular fields and are certain to produce a better result (quality of candidate, quality of short-list) than if the organization was to do the work itself.

- Marketing agencies are used as a fresh pool of ideas and to speed up the design and implementation of marketing campaigns. They are also a good source of consumer research statistics on buying and selling patterns.

- Software agencies are used to supply off-the-shelf packages or to design or refine these for particular applications. Relationships with software agencies also normally include training in the packages which have been bought.

- Production and production systems design agencies are used where the organization has a clear idea of what it needs to do but is less certain about how best to do it.

- Problem-solving agencies are used for handling crises such as arbitration in disputes, for handling industrial tribunal cases, for rectifying serious breakdowns, for handling serious public relations problems, and for putting right emergencies and crises. They are normally extremely expensive; but in return for this, they undertake to put the matter right or mitigate the damage quickly and effectively.

Notes

1. For all activities carried out by outsiders, some form of *service level arrangement* is essential. This is to ensure that both parties know where they stand at the outset and the basis on which satisfaction is achieved and fees are paid. This is either a *service level contract* in which everything is itemized and specified, or a *service level agreement* in which a broader remit is given and received and which again states or strongly indicates the acceptable level of performance.

2. When using outsiders it is usual to pay a proportion of the fee at the point of initial agreement. A further proportion is payable on completion of the work. The final instalment is normally delayed until between three and six months after completion. This is to ensure that what was undertaken really works. This fee structure

may be divided into equal parts, though increasingly organizations are adopting a 25–25–50 approach, with half the fee kept back in order to prove that what was proposed really works.

3.   Problems with subcontractors arise most often when there are misunderstandings over the volume and quality of work required.

4.   If fee levels are too low, good subcontractors will be driven out of the area. Poor contractors only will be available.

5.   Subcontracting incurs the attention of the Inland Revenue. Regular subcontracting, especially by individuals, is increasingly likely to be deemed to constitute employee status and organizations may be ordered to put these people on their payroll.

Summary

Organizations and their managers must ensure that, whoever is employed on whatever basis, they receive the same basic treatment. Part-time working has traditionally been viewed as a low status, secondary form of employment. This is a negative and divisive attitude.

The hours worked by individuals should be long enough to produce effective work, regular enough to build successful working relationships, and flexible enough to accommodate personal preferences and commitments.

Structuring and maintaining effective flexible work requires planning and consideration at the outset because this is to form the basis of the organization's structure, and product and service delivery. Proper planning also ensures that any changes are much more easily accommodated than constantly working hand to mouth.

When outsiders and subcontractors are used they must conform to required organization norms, patterns of behaviour and conduct.

The whole purpose is to give the organization strength in dealing with its customers and carrying out its activities. Staff and expertise can be drawn from a wide range of backgrounds, bringing with them talents, qualities and capabilities that would not otherwise be available.

The main lesson lies in understanding the opportunities and constraints of different patterns of work, how these can be harnessed and to whom they can be applied in particular situations.

3 Contractual arrangements

Contracts of Employment

A contract of employment exists once an offer of work has been made and accepted. This is normally confirmed in writing. All employees are bound by contracts of employment, whatever their length of service or hours worked. A contract of employment consists of the following.

Stated Terms

- The letter of offer of employment which must state:

    - the name and address of the employer;

    - the name of the employee;

    - where work is to be carried out;

    - the title of the job;

    - the hours to be worked;

    - rates and methods of pay;

    - other benefits (e.g. entitlements to paid holidays, membership of BUPA, use of company car and other equipment);

    - any specific obligations (e.g. uniform, other dress code, requirements to be trained and developed).

- Organizational procedures and practices:

    - staff handbooks;

    - collective agreements;

    - discipline, grievance and dismissal arrangements;

    - health and safety and emergency procedures.

- Other written information:

    - the content of the job advertisement;

-     –   organizational particulars and information;

-     –   any other organization papers which indicate particular ways of working, standards, expectations and impressions.

- Any information given orally:

  -     –   at interview;

  -     –   in other general discussions;

  -     –   in any other way, at any other time.

Implied Terms

- Implications of the job title and description. For example, there is a common understanding of the duties of a secretary, a supervisor, a manager, a cashier, a cleaner, as well as distinctive organizational requirements. How the work is to be carried out is reinforced at the induction stage.

- Required attitudes and approaches which are normally made clear at induction.

- Customer practice, indicating the reality of the working environment.

- Obligations:

  -     –   **employer:** to provide adequate equipment for the work to be carried out effectively; to provide workplace insurance; to provide suitable training and development; to set and maintain standards of care, behaviour and attitudes; to indicate modes of address; to treat everybody equally and fairly;

  -     –   **employee:** to work to the best of capabilities; to carry out stated and implied duties as directed or requested; to act in a safe and responsible manner at all times; to act in the employer's best interests.

- Expectations:

  -     –   **employer:** employers are entitled to expect that if someone has applied for a job, they are basically capable and qualified to do it. They are entitled to end the contract if it becomes clear that the employee is not capable;

–   **employee:** the employee is entitled to expect that the work to be done is as stated or implied in the job advertisement, job description and other information. They are entitled to sue for breach of contract if it becomes clear that this is not the case.

Flexible Contracts

The contractual form used is as described above. Particulars of flexible arrangements – hours, location, nature of work – are written in as appropriate, together with details of any additional obligations or requirements (e.g. expenses for travelling to different locations, different payment rates applying to various duties).

Flexibility of work and/or hours is made clear at the outset, and stated in the contract, so that everyone knows where they stand. If there is the certainty, likelihood or possibility that work, location or hours may change, this also is made clear at the outset.

Ideally the contract is presented to new employees at the commencement of employment. They should be taken through it point by point. Any problems or difficulties are resolved at the outset. It is then signed by the new employee and an employer's representative. Again, everyone is then clear where they stand.

The contract should be of a standard format held on disk. Individual particulars are then inserted in the usual way. Enough space is left on the standard format to enable:

- hours

- duties

- locations

- any other certain, likely or possible variations

to be inserted according to the particular agreement. In this way, bureaucracy and administration are kept to a minimum. The whole can then be transferred to the file of the new employee.

Notes

1.   ***Varying the contract***
Contracts may be changed or varied at any time as the result of operational necessity. The purpose is to come to an arrangement that is satisfactory, both to employer and employee.

The minimum period of consultation for this purpose required by law is four weeks. This is greatly extended if a major rearrangement is required – such as relocation or a significant change of occupation, working days or hours.

Employers are required to act fairly and reasonably in all cases. Where flexible contracts and flexible working are clearly the norm, there is a much greater latitude and freedom to manoeuvre than where these are rigid.

As long as adequate and suitable assistance and training are provided, consultation is carried out, and operational necessity is demonstrated, employees are required to accede to any variations.

2.   *Terminating the contract*

The usual reasons for termination are:

–   persistent breaches of discipline;

–   gross misconduct (instances and examples of gross misconduct should always be indicated);

–   lack of capability to do the job;

–   where work has ceased or diminished (i.e. redundancy);

–   some other substantial reason (such as incurring a jail sentence or serious illness which makes it impossible to continue to work).

Under flexible working, the main consideration is redundancy. It is both expensive and demoralizing to all staff when redundancies occur. The purpose of engaging the flexible approach is to have a fully capable, multi-skilled and positive workforce. The attitude must be that redundancy is only to be used as a last resort. If people have shown themselves willing and able to be retrained, redeployed and moved around in the past, this is a much better alternative when one form of work ceases or diminishes.

There are legal requirements to consult on redundancies as soon as possible and specific periods according to the numbers affected.

3.   *Equality of treatment*

By law, as well as a matter of common sense, everyone is entitled to basic equality of treatment, regardless of length of service or hours worked.

Basic standards of attitude and behaviour should apply to all. First name terms should ideally apply across the entire organization as the formality of surname or job title terms is in itself a barrier to full flexibility. It also smacks of tradition – the way things were done – rather than flexibility – the way things should now be done.

Basic terms and conditions should apply to all. If one person has to clock or sign in, this should apply to all. There should be one staff handbook, one set of rules and procedures, and again these are to apply to everyone. Apart from anything else, this greatly reduces the administrative and bureaucratic burden.

Any view that is taken that some jobs, functions, departments or divisions are 'more important' necessarily means that others are 'less important'. It is a negative attitude, directly and immediately affecting those in the 'less important' areas. It also affects those in the 'more important' areas who take steps and use resources to protect and enhance their position rather than in the pursuit of profitable and effective activities.

This does not mean equality of salary. Differentials are clearly made on the basis of expertise, responsibility, authority and hours worked. Differentials should never be made on any other basis.

Discrimination on grounds of victimization, harassment or bullying should normally at least be a disciplinary offence, and many organizations list this under gross misconduct. Discrimination on grounds of race, ethnic origin, sex/gender, religion, marital status, membership/refusal to join a trade union and spent convictions (with some exceptions) is illegal.

Opportunities for variety, training and development, project work and secondments are made available to everyone based on capability and potential, regardless of length of service or hours worked. Under flexible working, this is arranged through a combination of organization demand, personal preference and interest, and professional, technical and occupational expertise.

Differentials in relative status and value are avoided if everyone is treated in this way and put on the same basic terms and conditions and standards of attitude and behaviour.

Fixed-Term Contracts

Fixed-term contracts are the same as normal contracts of employment, except that the date on which the contract is to end is stated. Fixed-term

contracts may be of any duration suitable to the organization – for example, some local government bodies and health authorities place their senior managers on fixed-term contracts of up to seven years. The date of termination is stated at the outset of employment and is normally:

- a specified date in the future;

- an indicated date – for example, in a fixed-term contract covering maternity leave, it is permissible to use the phrase 'when employee X returns from maternity leave';

- where the contract is for the duration of a project, it is usual to use the phrase 'when the project ends'.

Notes

1. For any contract that lasts more than two years a redundancy or severance payment is normally required at the end. Employees can be persuaded to waive their rights to this, but it is usual to make some form of payment in return. In any case, employees must know what they are doing, and why, and must not be coerced or cajoled down this route. Failure to do this normally constitutes breach of contract.

2. For any fixed-term contract that is renewed so that the total period of continuous employment is more than two years, a redundancy or severance payment is usually required as above.

3. If an employee breaks a fixed-term contract (i.e. leaves before it ends), it is open for the employer to sue him or her for breach of contract. However, this rarely occurs in practice because of the time, expense, inconvenience and (invariably) adverse publicity involved.

4. If an employee on a fixed-term contract is clearly not up to the standard required it is possible to cancel the contract on the grounds that the employee has breached it because of their lack of capability. The onus is placed entirely on the employer to prove this. If standards and capabilities are not clearly specified, the employee is placed in a strong position to defend the cancellation. Where the case goes against the employer, the courts normally make an award to the employee of the equivalent of the rest of their entitlement under the terms of the contract.

5. Where it becomes essential to extend the fixed-term contract – for example, where a project is not completed to time or where

maternity leave has been extended for some reason – it is quite legitimate to do this on a week-by-week or month-by-month basis. However, once again, any extension that takes the period of continuous employment over two years normally incurs obligations to pay redundancy or severance at the end.

6.   For fixed-term contracts, it is both useful and legitimate to make some form of bonus or additional final payment at the end of the contract. This is only payable upon satisfactory completion by the employee. The final payment can take one of two forms.

– **An additional payment.** This means that effectively the employee is being overpaid. The trade-off for this is the fact that the employee is no longer retained on the payroll and has no longer to be accommodated or provided with equipment and services. The additional payment may therefore be seen as a relatively small price to pay.

– **Money withheld over the period of the contract pending its satisfactory completion.** Withholding may be overt or covert. The overt form is where both parties have agreed to this beforehand. The covert is where the withholding is presented to the employee as a bonus, but where what has really happened is that the employer has offered the employee the contract based on a lesser wage or salary, and that only by achieving the bonus do they make 100% of what the employer is prepared to pay.

Any form of final payment should be stated and understood at the commencement of employment.

Subcontracting

Contracts for subcontractors do not constitute a contract of employment. They concentrate entirely on the level, volume and quality of product or service required. It is usual simply to specify at the outset of the contract:

- the fee structure;

- the volume of work;

- the quality required;

- the duration of the contract;

- how performance and satisfaction are to be assessed.

How the work is carried out is a matter for the subcontractor. It is both necessary and quite legitimate for regular progress meetings to be convened. It is also essential to have general and continuing effective liaison and communication. Within standards of attitude, behaviour and performance which are specified and the norms at the contracting organization, subcontracted work is carried out by the subcontractor in ways which they see fit.

Notes

1.   Contract timescales have to be sufficiently long to give the relationship a chance to work effectively; this has to be balanced against the threat of being tied into an expensive and unproductive relationship.

2.   Where there is a change from employee to self-employed status, the ex-employee becomes responsible for his/her tax, national insurance and the keeping of accounts. The ex-employee is also likely to have to provide his/her own equipment in the future. There is no security of tenure and no obligation (on either part) for any contract to be reviewed once completed. There is at least a moral responsibility on the employer to make all of this clear.

3.   All subcontracting arrangements may legitimately be varied by agreement between the two parties.

4.   Subcontractors may not be prevented from carrying out activities elsewhere provided that these do not interfere with the particular contract. The only exception to this is where commercial confidentiality or a conflict of interest is considered to be present; the onus is entirely on the contracting organization to prove this.

Employment Law

All employees are entitled to employment protection after two years' continuous service whatever the hours worked. Anyone – whether designated full-time or part-time – may claim unfair dismissal if they lose their job for no good or demonstrable reason after two years' continuous service.

All employees are entitled not to be victimized or discriminated against on grounds of race, gender, disability, membership of a trade union, refusal to join a trade union or a spent conviction for a criminal offence, regardless of length of service or hours worked.

All female employees are entitled to 14 weeks' maternity leave if they become pregnant, regardless of length of service or hours worked. All female employees of more than two years' continuous service are entitled to 29 weeks' maternity leave regardless of hours worked. All pregnant employees are entitled to return to their old job or one not substantially different and on the same pay, terms and conditions of employment as when they left. If the pay has risen in the meantime, they are entitled to the new rate.

All employees are entitled to one week's notice after four weeks' continuous employment regardless of hours worked. If the contract specifies more than this, then the higher amount must be given.

All employees are entitled to fair treatment in cases of discipline, grievance and dismissal, regardless of length of service or hours worked. They must be given the opportunity to hear the case against them and state their point of view. They are entitled to representation at each stage. They are entitled to receive confirmation in writing of the decision and to appeal against this if they so wish.

Conclusions

The distinction between full- and part-time employment is becoming ever more blurred. There is now no set number of hours which is deemed to constitute a full-time job. Guidelines issued by the Department for Employment and the Advisory, Conciliation and Arbitration Service in 1995 recommend that all employees are treated exactly the same regardless of length of service or hours worked. This is normally the benchmark for questions that arise over 'fairness and reasonableness of treatment' and 'best practice'.

It is also clear that many hitherto part-time broken or intermittent contracts are now regarded in law as continuous employment. This is now more or less certain where agreed periods of unpaid leave are taken – for example, with term time and other 'hours around children' employment patterns. Employers which allow their employees periods of extended leave, sabbaticals and career breaks must acknowledge the period of continuous service when the employee returns to work.

It is likely that the period of exclusion from employment protection will be reduced from two years to one year in the near future. If and when this occurs, it is certain to apply to all employees whatever their hours of work or pattern of employment.

4　Management issues

Introduction

The first duty of all organizations in managing flexible working is to engender the right attitudes and approaches of its managers and supervisors. Where flexibility is based on part-time, fixed-term contracts and job-sharing type work, the approach that demeans – 'They are only part-timers' and 'They are only job sharers' – is unacceptable. It is absolutely certain that if people are treated as 'only' something, this is how they will turn out. Work, profitability, productivity, effectiveness and customer service are all certain to suffer. Moreover, this attitude is certain to spread to other full-time staff who will regard themselves as superior. It will then spread to part-timers who are likely to develop some form of siege mentality. They are certain to develop defensive and negative attitudes. The result again, is to affect effectiveness and profitability.

All employees, whatever their hours of work or length of service, are to be treated fairly and equally. Any departure from this line is punished. Any failure to do this is certain to result in grievances, and court and industrial tribunal cases which are all costly and debilitating.

The management task is therefore to produce excellent and top quality staff who make excellent products and give high levels of service. This is the source of customer satisfaction, repeat business, enhanced reputation – and profits.

Management Style

Flexible working is best supported by an open, honest and visible style of management and supervision. This is especially important where large numbers of part-time staff are present, and where people move around regularly between different tasks during the work periods. Visibility builds the trust and empathy essential in any effective working relationship. For part-timers and those who do move around, this has to be built quickly.

Honesty and openness are also critical. Very often, there is an organizational issue at stake. The organization itself must first learn the difference between being open and not – and the benefits of the former and the drawbacks of the latter. In many cases, organizations lose sight of the reasons why certain things are kept confidential. While confidentiality clearly extends to

customer bases and profiles, new products, services and initiatives and other operational brainwaves, there is very little else that needs this approach. The more that is kept from the staff, the more they conclude that the organization is hiding something.

A substantial part of the management job consists therefore of 'walking the job'. Where this is not possible – for example, where employees work from home or in regional centres – regular and positive telephone contacts are to be maintained. This should be supported by regular meetings.

Regular meetings are also essential where there is a large measure of contact through e-mail and fax. This breaks down physical and psychological barriers and enhances identity.

The priority is attention to operational requirements and the patterns of staffing necessary to make these effective.

Administration and procedures are to be kept as simple as possible. There is an administrative workload generated by the variety of work patterns indicated and used. This is accommodated by standardizing and simplifying as much as possible, especially forms of contract of employment and work procedures. Use and adherence to procedures is kept to a minimum, reserved for serious issues only. Smaller problems and issues are resolved by the work group, managers and supervisors on the spot. This frees up both time and resources for the primary purpose of pursuing customer satisfaction and product and service excellence. It also removes the need for industrial relations, staff management and other administrative superstructures and subfunctions; and this again frees up resources for more positive and productive purposes.

Procedures for the handling of disciplinary and grievance matters should be kept as simple as possible. They should be used as infrequently as possible – because managers and supervisors have the capability of resolving issues before recourse to procedures is necessary. Where it is necessary to invoke procedures, strict time constraints should be imposed. This prevents issues from festering, from people taking sides, from battle lines being drawn. The purpose is to get operations back on a successful and effective footing as quickly as possible. The vast majority of grievances will be resolved on the spot. Where procedures are invoked, this should take no longer than two weeks.

Disciplinary matters should follow the same pattern. The only constraint is to allow the employee time to prepare his/her response to an issue and to seek representation and support for his/her point of view. This is also the approach for reporting relationships between departments and senior management. Information required and provided should be suitable and effective. Continuous attention should be paid to the volumes and quality of

information available, and the purposes to which it is put. Regular requirements – for example, for year end – are clearly signalled and structured into departmental workloads. Information systems should be designed and commissioned with the demands and requirements in mind in order to eliminate crisis requests, overloads and underloads.

Interdepartmental relations and relationships between operational and senior management are based on organizational effectiveness rather than adherence to procedures. Problems that do arise are to be resolved quickly and effectively, again with the emphasis on product and service quality and customer satisfaction. Where the issues concern staff, procedures must be followed and these are to be kept simple and effective.

Management Qualities

For flexible working the main qualities required are:

- enthusiasm, commitment, dedication;

- understanding of what constitutes effective performance and commitment to achieving and improving this;

- knowledge and understanding of the pressures, opportunities, constraints and drives present in the workplace; of those that can and cannot be controlled; of other constraints in which work is to be carried out;

- leadership, communication and decision-making capabilities, based on staff expectations and demands;

- knowing and understanding what constitutes successful and effective performance; the ability to take remedial action quickly when performance falls short; handling staff, production, service and customer problems when they arise.

Management Training

Training in the skills and qualities needed to manage the flexible workforce consists of the following.

- Ensuring that managers and supervisors have positive attitudes and dispositions towards their staff; ensuring that managers and

supervisors understand what constitutes customer satisfaction and expectations and the nature and quality of activities necessary to achieve this.

- Developing interpersonal skills, as much of the supervision and management routines are concerned with promoting understanding; harmonizing people on a variety of working arrangements; consultation and briefings; solving questions and problems without recourse to procedures.

- Developing high standards of communication, both written and spoken.

- Developing managerial and supervisory habits of 'walking the job' (also known as managing by walking about).

- Training in practical problem-solving in all activities – product and service quality, customer issues, staff and personal matters and questions. The emphasis is on quick and effective solutions with which those directly affected are satisfied and that can be accommodated within the wider organization.

- Appraisal of knowledge and skills, based on continuous assessment of performance with regular formal or semi-formal meetings. Regular staff appraisals need not and should not take long; most of the work is best done as part of the continuous working relationship. Again, problems become apparent early and are easily nipped in the bud. This is especially essential when managing part-timers and outworkers with whom regular face-to-face contact is limited. It is damaging to both production, quality and morale if issues are allowed to drag on without being resolved.

- Discipline and grievance based on establishing and maintaining standards of working relationship that keep both to a minimum. Management and supervisory training in these areas is concerned with equipping those involved with the capabilities and autonomy to resolve issues before they become problems. Providing training in the operation of simple, direct and speedy procedures indicated elsewhere is in the context of maintaining staff morale and effectiveness.

- Continuous regular briefings concerning organizational, departmental, divisional, group and individual performance with the emphasis on the positive and the early identification and resolution of problems.

- Knowledge and understanding of all aspects of organizational operations and activities; where the individual manager or supervisor fits in; the nature of their required contribution; familiarity with the work of related departments; understanding required performance targets; understanding the constraints within which they have to work.

Management training and development is a continued requirement. Some is clearly best pursued in-house. The pursuit of external courses and formal qualifications is also highly desirable because it broadens the general perspective and understanding of managers; it enables them to come into contact with managers from other organizations, bringing fresh ideas to bear on existing issues and problems, and develops the fund of knowledge and talent available in the organization.

Management Performance

Effective management of flexible working requires high quality and distinctive forms of expertise, based on the style indicated above and for which initial and continuous training is required. The manager or supervisor is the point of reference for all staff – whatever their length of service, level of expertise or hours worked. Their people look to them for quick and effective decisions, solutions to problems, and the creation of an effective, positive and productive place of work.

The elements of managerial performance are:

- setting and maintaining the required attitudes and values, reinforcing these through personal conduct and performance and remedying these where they fall short;

- setting goals, aims and objectives for the department or division as a whole and for teams, groups and individuals within it;

- delegating, giving autonomy, authority and responsibilities to subordinates to complete work as they see fit;

- enabling and supporting the pursuit of projects and initiatives;

- improving and developing the expertise of all staff;

- controlling the work and performance of persons with a variety of different expertise, experience, hours and patterns of work;

- acting as advocate and spokesperson for the department and its members;

- being receptive, evaluative and judgemental of ideas received from members of staff;

- continuously seeking for improvements to product and service quality, and for improvements to work methods and practices;

- involvement in and with the staff in the choice of new production technology, work methods and practices;

- enhancing the department's recognition and achievement.

Effective flexible work management is dependent upon individual managers and supervisors having the capabilities and qualities to carry this out. It is also dependent upon having high quality staff.

High Quality Staff

High quality staff are either attracted from outside or produced and grown from within.

Outside

The benefit of recruiting from outside is to bring in fresh talent, skills, knowledge and expertise. Attitudes and behaviour are formed and developed at the commencement of employment.

Outsiders are also used to bring fresh life or impetus to existing activities.

Once inside, outsiders are trained and developed according to the organization's policies and practices.

The problems normally lie in the length of time the recruitment and selection processes take (several months for some appointments, especially management, technical and professional), and in the length of time it takes to make them fully effective in their new roles (which is the drive behind all effective induction programmes and activities).

Growing Your Own

Growing your own means that organizations get the staff that they need and want. This extends especially to attitudes and behaviour. It greatly contributes to staff motivation. It is a mark of the value placed on the staff and the organization's commitment to them.

The main drawback is the length of time that this takes. Growing your own is a long-term and continuous commitment. It also tends to promote introspection and elitism if it does not include activities away from the organization (e.g. training and development courses off-site).

The best approach is clearly a mixture of the two. This is based on an understanding and evaluation of the specific benefits of growth and development and where the needs for fresh impetus lie. Emphasis is also needed on the integration of outsiders as quickly and effectively as possible.

Continuous Improvement and Development

This is a reflection of the required commitment to training and development. It covers improving the ways in which current activities are carried out. It also means reviewing, refining, streamlining and restructuring bureaucracy and administration where necessary. It also includes project work, work improvement activities, attention to quality, secondments and off-site activities, as well as on-the-job training.

Job Titles

The great majority of job titles tend to limit and pigeonhole people into restrictive and restricted positions. They create inflexibility of themselves. Many job titles also demean the job holder, especially in semi-skilled and unskilled areas. For example, it is not unusual to hear people say 'I'm only a secretary' or 'I'm only a checkout operator', and if individuals themselves think that they are 'only' something, then the organization is likely to regard them in this way also.

This also happens to others elsewhere on organization maps and ladders. There is relative status accorded to and within personnel, marketing and finance functions, for example, through the use of job titles such as 'Junior Personnel Officer', 'Finance Assistant' or 'Marketing Executive'.

As well as generally being restricting, this form of title tends to put a dampener on the enthusiasm of job holders and to indicate boundaries of responsibility, authority and activity which are not to be crossed.

There are also the pigeonholes for the un-pigeonholeable. At their most positive, titles such as 'Project Officer' or 'Manager of Corporate Affairs' tend to be allocated to those whose remits do not sit easily within an organization structure or hierarchy. This tends again to reinforce any general lack of flexibility. At its most negative (and much more common) is the tendency to use such titles for those for whom no real job exists. And nobody is fooled – not the rest of the organization, not the work colleagues and certainly not the job holder.

Some organizations have tried to get over this by introducing much more generic and (supposedly) positive titles such as 'crew member', 'cast member' or 'staff member'. Others have gone further still and allowed people to invent their own job titles. In the most extreme cases, this is fanciful and silly, but it does at least indicate that people are not to be bounded by restrictive job titles.

Japanese companies tend to go along the line of promoting company identity (rather than job identity). Employees tend therefore to say 'I work for Mitsubishi' and 'I work for Honda' rather than 'I am a technician' or 'I am a supervisor'. This flexibility is borne out by operational work practices which require the employees to work anywhere that the company requires and (at its best) removes the words 'That is not my job' from the employee's vocabulary.

Job Descriptions

Under flexible working, job descriptions encompass and reconcile the following:

- organizational requirements of transferability and moveability – especially from quiet areas to those of heavy demand;

- personal requirements of job holders;

  - pursuing the career or occupation with which they are concerned and to which they are committed;

  - enlarging their capabilities;

  - ensuring that work is not too bitty or fragmented;

  - meeting personal expectations.

The standpoint taken is that everyone is to be prepared to do anything, at any time. Rather than itemizing tasks, the approach is to emphasize the need to 'work as directed' and 'work as required'.

This is shorter and more positive than the traditional method of itemizing each and every task that may be required of the job holder. It is much easier to understand. It is a better basis for a positive, productive and effective working relationship. It is also far less bureaucratic. It places on managers and supervisors the responsibility for organizing and directing work from a positive and meaningful point of view.

In cases where it is necessary to emphasize or indicate the range of work to be carried out, a list of tasks is added to the end of the description. There will

also always be the rider that this list is not exhaustive and may be added to or changed at any time by agreement and with consultation.

The result is to greatly reduce the number of job titles, especially those that tend to limit or demean (see above).

Person Specifications

The person specification is a statement of the qualities and expertise required. In flexible working, the emphasis is on positive attitudes, a willingness to learn and develop, dynamism and responsiveness, as well as skill and capability. 'Want to do' and 'Will do' become as important as 'Can do'. There are also related qualities of creativity, innovation and interest.

It is quite legitimate to ask for these qualities in job advertisements, as well as indicating particular qualifications, skills and knowledge content. Those who genuinely hold these qualities are normally in great demand. They expect to be able to use these qualities in this kind of work, and do not stay long where they are not in fact required.

Testing for attitudes and enthusiasm is carried out through:

- personality tests, which indicate the presence of these qualities;

- problem-solving tests, in which the attitude (as well as the solution) to the problem is observed;

- establishing the reasons why the individual wants to come and work for the company;

- participation in group discussions established for the purpose;

- in-tray exercises and 'work under pressure tests', which again enable the attitude (as well as the approach) to be observed;

- inferences from a person's general demeanour.

Notes

1.   Organizations that continue to use traditional and well understood job titles must recognize that job holders will expect their work content to continue to reflect these. 'Manager' implies some form of executive responsibility. 'Secretary' implies typing, administration, filing and some office practice. If the work is to be very different from this, then the job title should be changed so that potential employees are not disappointed when they start.

2.   If there are bad or boring activities, then these should be made clear at the outset and should be shared around as far as possible. Flexibility is not an excuse to dump all the bad bits on a new starter.

Selection

Selection concentrates on the key qualities identified in the person specification. The emphasis of any selection activity will be geared towards the identification of the required attitudes as much as the skill, knowledge and expertise. The view taken is that an effective flexible worker is a combination of expertise and attitude rather than a person with the highest level of expertise. In these circumstances, it is invariably better to take on someone who can do the job *and who wants to do it*, than someone who is clearly an expert in the area but cannot always be bothered.

Induction

Successful flexible working is dependent upon effective induction. The required attitudes and values are reinforced during the induction period. Emphasis is also placed on getting the employee to carry out their expertise *in the ways required*. The length of induction, its priority, the attention paid to it by managers and supervisors, as well as the content of the induction programme, are all critical to its successful outcome. The main thrust again is to build the foundations for the working relationship of the future.

This is important for all staff whatever their jobs and work. Some organizations neglect the induction of part-time and unskilled staff because they are 'only' part-time and unskilled – and so, again, the message given is the 'only' description. There is no real chance of a fully productive relationship. Others neglect the induction of management, technological and administrative staff on the grounds that anyone with these skills and expertise should be able to find their own way into the job. This is also a negative approach. At the very best it takes longer to build up an effective working relationship. At the worst, it is alienating and destructive. Those affected will take refuge in their expertise, rather than building identity with the organization and their colleagues.

None of this means taking a long time over induction. It does mean using the time available to best effect. It means identifying and concentrating on those things that are important to the individual – any individual – at the outset of any employment – identity, familiarity and early achievement. Those things that are important to the organization – positive attitudes, willingness to work – stem from this, and will follow once the others are right.

For all staff, whatever their location or pattern of working, frequency of attendance or hours of work, the following is essential:

- beginning the development of a positive and productive working relationship with the supervisor or manager, and establishing the ways in which this is to be conducted;

- familiarization with the environment, procedures and practices;

- meeting work colleagues and building the occupational network, personal relationships, mutual trust and confidence;

- developing the required attitudes and values, standards of behaviour and performance;

- putting right any initial misconceptions or misunderstandings.

Time and trouble taken at the outset prevent misunderstandings occurring later. Where problems do subsequently occur, they are not then the result of anything that could have been put right earlier or prevented from happening altogether.

Job Training

Organizations that want flexible working must be prepared to train their staff initially, regularly and continuously. Employees coming into flexible working situations must be prepared to undertake training on the same basis. This applies to everyone, at all levels of authority, skill and responsibility.

Production

Production staff are trained in all the necessary aspects – each workstation, volume and quality control, every part of the process from input of raw materials to output of finished goods. It also includes how to put right minor breakages and stoppages. It must include a quick and easily accessible point of reference to get repairs carried out when the machinery breaks down – and the authority to do this.

It includes training for the future, to identify and develop potential, to prepare for new technologies that are likely to come along.

Service

For service staff, the approach is similar. This normally includes customer service and public relations skills. It also invariably includes the understanding and usage of information and communications technology.

Again, there are elements of training for the future in both technology advances and service improvements.

Notes

1.   For all these, there are elements of responsibility, and the formation of positive, dynamic and committed attitudes.

2.   Some production companies have abolished quality control functions altogether. Customer complaints are referred back directly to the team or individual which produced the item in question. The onus and responsibility is placed on each team or individual to avoid these problems so that they are not faced with customer complaints. Any further problem will be referred to a senior level of management who will then question them also.

3.   One restaurant chain has abolished the jobs of restaurant manager, head waiter, restaurant cashier and restaurant purchasing officer at each of its locations. The scheduling and arrangement of tables is worked out among the waiters and waitresses and one of these will also take responsibility for cashing up at the end of the day before they all go home. The purchasing of food is carried out by the chef. The purchasing and ordering of drink is carried out by the bar staff. This has resulted in enhanced job interest and job satisfaction, and the use and development of potential – and earnings. It also meant attention to extensive job training and continued development of those involved.

4.   Qualifications. Some organizations provide the means for some of their staff to pursue qualifications. Others provide this for all staff. Others still insist that their people study something – whether directly work-related or not. These qualifications may be at any level, from basic, professional, technical and business skills (at GNVQ Levels 1 and 2 for example), through to release for Masters' Degrees and Diplomas at universities and colleges.

              Whatever the level, distinctive improvements and enlargements of expertise are achieved. It also acts as a vehicle for unlocking potential and enthusiasm and generating much higher levels of expectation and performance all round.

              Some companies have had their in-house training programmes put on a formalized basis, leading to recognized qualifications at the end. Completion of these is compulsory and a condition of continuing employment.

Some companies pay for evening classes – again, whether work-related or not. They take the view that any development and any participation in organized activities is better than none. It also demonstrates the organization's wider general interest in their people.

Motivation

Work motivation is based on:

- demanding, interesting, varied and valuable work that people are capable of carrying out; recognizing and rewarding their achievements; taking early remedial action when standards fall;

- treating everyone equally and with respect; creating workplace relationships based on trust, honesty, openness and integrity; creating a unity of purpose and mutual interest between organization and staff; developing positive work, professional and personal relationships within and between groups;

- attending to individual needs, wants, drives, hopes, fears and aspirations; ensuring that everyone progresses, develops and improves operationally, professionally and personally;

- high, regular and increasing levels of pay.

If all of this is in place, organizations are entitled to expect high quality, high value work. Creating these conditions is the organization's responsibility. The potential for this is much greater under flexible working arrangements because so many more of the conditions are easier to satisfy. Moreover, people are coming into flexible working with raised expectations of security, employability, variety and opportunity. The basis of the whole relationship is clear – and positive.

Motivation is adversely affected by:

- management style and the invisibility of managers and supervisors; inability to solve problems quickly; adversarial approaches to staff;

- physical and psychological distance, based again on visibility and also on forms of preferential treatment, inaccessibility and uncertainty;

- bad interpersonal and interoccupational relationships;

- boring and valueless work;

- bad and unclear communications, infrequently delivered and frequently changed, and where the message given does not relate to the reality of the situation;

- inherent dishonesty, lack of integrity and unfairness in the treatment of people.

It should also be noted that individual motivation changes as the relationship between people and their organization progresses. The motivation required:

- to apply for a job

- to turn up for interview

- to accept a job

- to turn up on the first day

- to turn up on the second day

- to keep turning up

is different in each case. The individual is affected by the ways in which they have been treated on each of these occasions and their motivation is either enhanced or diminished accordingly.

Under flexible working, motivation is most likely to be adversely affected by pay levels, and the quality or the value of the work.

Where pay is low, it is a mark of low esteem and value. It reflects the level of worth placed on the staff. The only exception to this is voluntary or vocational work – and vocation should never be confused with professionalism or expertise. It is both unfair and unethical to take advantage of people's commitment to their customers and clients.

Where work value is low jobs – and therefore staff – are dispensable and those involved will know this better than anyone. Work of low value is extravagant and wasteful and is either to be abolished or improved.

Where product and service quality is low, there is no personal, professional or occupational feeling of satisfaction from being involved. Indeed, there is often a desire not to be associated. Real achievement is based on completing

things that are good and positive and give satisfaction, not just on completing something.

People's motivation is directly affected by:

- **expectations:** the outcomes that they anticipate as the result of being in a situation and carrying out work;

- **efforts:** the amount of energy that they are prepared to put into the situation;

- **rewards:** the benefits to be accrued by being in the particular situation.

Recognizing the balance between the three is vital. If rewards do not match expectations, efforts decline. If other expectations are not met, efforts decline. If rewards exceed expectations, efforts increase in the short term, though in the long term this becomes the new level of expectation.

Individuals – whatever their pattern of work or frequency of attendance – therefore act best when they have a reasonable expectation that their effort will lead to the desired rewards and outcomes. It also emphasizes the importance of the individual in any form of working relationship. It also indicates that raising expectations leads to the anticipation of enhanced rewards, and that lowering rewards reduces both expectations and effort.

Communication and Understanding

Communication and understanding are the other main keys to staff motivation. The nature, media, language, volume and quality of communications reinforces the working relationship. Again, where one or more of these elements is lacking or wrong, motivation suffers.

Communication is best and most effective face to face, supported in writing in clear, simple, direct language. Communication always suffers when this is not present. It is also damaged when it is not supported by managerial or organizational actions or integrity. When this occurs, people always look for hidden meanings and messages. This is counter-productive to effective work, damaging and ultimately destroying working relationships.

Where face-to-face communication is not possible (e.g. for homeworkers, sales staff and others working away from the organization for long periods), regular meetings are convened to get over the problems caused by working in isolation. These meetings should devote at least part of their time to general discussions about the overall state of affairs and filling in the

outworkers on any and all matters of importance, general knowledge and concern. It is also the opportunity to ensure that achievements and successes are noted and recognized. Attendance at these meetings is compulsory. It is the only clear opportunity that organizations and their managers have of building on existing levels of confidence and identity, as well as resolving problems and points of contention. *Serious problems should always be tackled face to face.* To attempt to tackle them by e-mail or over the telephone or by fax normally results in the situation getting worse.

These conditions are present in all effective flexible working. Motivation of the flexible workforce is completed by:

- good and positive supervision which encourages and enhances rather than restricts;

- work satisfaction, based on flexible structuring, enrichment and variety;

- high levels of team, group and organizational identity;

- positive and professional relationships between group members and different groups and teams;

- recognition for work well done;

- recognizing communication problems that are likely to arise in specific situations and devising patterns of supervision and the means of communication that address these to best effect;

- an attitude that learns from failure rather than seeks to apportion blame;

- attention to the general working environment, adequate standards of accommodation and cleanliness, a standard of facilities with which people can be comfortable;

- relating status to work performance and organization membership rather than to job titles, group or department membership.

If all of this is in place, organizations are entitled to expect a reciprocal commitment from their employees, high levels of that commitment and high standards and quality of work.

Notes

1.   **Fixed-term contracts**
      Problems often arise with fixed-term contracts when the staff member is coming to the end of the contract and there is no

outworkers on any and all matters of importance, general knowledge and concern. It is also the opportunity to ensure that achievements and successes are noted and recognized. Attendance at these meetings is compulsory. It is the only clear opportunity that organizations and their managers have of building on existing levels of confidence and identity, as well as resolving problems and points of contention. *Serious problems should always be tackled face to face.* To attempt to tackle them by e-mail or over the telephone or by fax normally results in the situation getting worse.

These conditions are present in all effective flexible working. Motivation of the flexible workforce is completed by:

- good and positive supervision which encourages and enhances rather than restricts;

- work satisfaction, based on flexible structuring, enrichment and variety;

- high levels of team, group and organizational identity;

- positive and professional relationships between group members and different groups and teams;

- recognition for work well done;

- recognizing communication problems that are likely to arise in specific situations and devising patterns of supervision and the means of communication that address these to best effect;

- an attitude that learns from failure rather than seeks to apportion blame;

- attention to the general working environment, adequate standards of accommodation and cleanliness, a standard of facilities with which people can be comfortable;

- relating status to work performance and organization membership rather than to job titles, group or department membership.

If all of this is in place, organizations are entitled to expect a reciprocal commitment from their employees, high levels of that commitment and high standards and quality of work.

Notes

1.   **Fixed-term contracts**
      Problems often arise with fixed-term contracts when the staff member is coming to the end of the contract and there is no

prospect of it being renewed. The main thrust is to ensure that the groundwork is done at the induction stage so that the individual concerned knows what is expected of him/her throughout the duration. This is supported by the 'final bonus' approach to pay (see page 24), where the money is only made up if the whole contract is completed satisfactorily. It is also supported by the style of supervision that (as with everything else) nips in the bud problems of attitude, behaviour or performance. From this point of view, fixed-term contract staff are no different to anyone else.

Those whose performance distinctly lapses in the last few months of the contract should be put through poor performance procedures as quickly as possible.

This either has the effect of raising performance or not. In the former case, well and good; in the latter, the organization has both grounds for terminating the contract forthwith and evidence to produce to defend any subsequent prosecution for breach of contract.

The ground rules are therefore clear at the outset. Fixed-term contract staff are treated exactly the same as anyone else. Opportunities afforded by the organization are open to fixed-term contract staff, the same as everyone else. The benefit lies in adopting a positive rather than a negative view.

When fixed-term contract staff are engaged for the duration of a project rather than a specified period of time and they finish the project early, it is often best to pay up the contract and let them go if there is nothing else that they can usefully be doing. A greater problem is likely to arise where a project overruns and one of the duties of project managers (and those who manage project managers) is to ensure that the work is not being deliberately spun out.

2. **Irregular work**
    Problems arise around the areas of identity, recognition and achievement. The best way to get over this is to make all part-time work as regular as possible. Where this is not possible, time needs to be found to integrate the irregular worker into the organization and with those with whom they have to work. It is often very difficult to build up a useful and positive working relationship when hours are too short or too infrequent; if this is the only approach possible in the circumstances, then the difficulty should be recognized and such steps as are possible in the circumstances taken.

3.   Some organizations compensate for dull, boring and unsatisfactory work by putting up wages, indeed overpaying. This only makes work more bearable, not more interesting. Indeed, it is counter-productive in some circumstances because people set themselves targets of gritting their teeth and working for a specific period of time to earn a set amount of money before quitting.

Dull, boring and unstretching work is also detrimental to both mental and physical health. Financial compensation therefore only addresses this problem in the short term. In the long term people leave anyway, and the performance of those who do stay declines as their health is affected, whatever the level of pay.

Where work is dull, boring and unsatisfactory, it should be restructured.

4.   Best results from staff are achieved through increased levels and requirements of commitment and achievement, and through the use of talents and qualities through the development and improvement of expertise, work methods and the working environment. Not to do this, ultimately has a detrimental standardizing effect on all routine aspects of work. Motivation and morale drop as does work interest – and this applies to all types of work and levels of expertise.

Pay and Benefits

High quality and flexible staff are well rewarded. This does not mean overpaying. It does mean paying as much as is feasible in the circumstances. Pay should also be increased to reflect improvements in levels of performance (especially organizational performance); expertise; and job enlargement, especially where additional responsibility is taken on.

Pay

The following elements of payment can be identified.

- **Payments:** annual, quarterly, monthly, four-weekly, weekly, daily, hourly; commission, bonus, increments, fees; profit, performance and merit-related elements.

- **Allowances:** attendance, disturbance, shift, weekend, unsocial hours, training and development, location and relocation, absence from home, special conditions – for example, dangerous and hazardous locations and occupations, other benefits and rewards.

Payment mixes adopted by organizations in devising and implementing reward strategies for different staff categories cover a variety of aims and purposes in response to particular situations. The general purpose is to address the following.

- **Expectations:** to meet the expectations of the job holder.

- **Attractiveness:** for the purposes of attracting and retaining staff.

- **Motivation:** based on value, effort, expertise and future commitment.

- **Mixes of payment with other aspects:** people in the UK expect to receive a 'reward package', a combination of pay with other benefits and rewards. This varies according to the particular situation.

- **Occupational aspects:** part of the reward package is likely to include the provision of specialist, expert and continuous training.

- **Performance and profit-related elements:** related either to the achievement of particular objectives, or to overall company performance.

  Where it is based on targets, the scheme must be believed in, valued and understood by all concerned. Targets must be achievable. They must be neither too easy nor too difficult. Targets must be set in advance; if they are achieved, payment must always be made. The purpose is to reward effort and achievement on the part of the staff.

Where pay is related to company profitability and performance, the best and fairest approach is to pay everyone the same percentage of their salary. For example, a 10% performance-related element would result in someone on £3,000 receiving a bonus of £300; for someone on £30,000, a bonus of £3,000 would be received; and so on.

Where performance is to be rewarded in the issuing of share options, this again should be on an equal basis. Share options should be available to anyone who wants to take advantage of them; where restrictions are placed, again this should be done as a percentage of individual salary.

Where pay is related to team performance, all members should receive the same percentage bonus.

Where pay is related to individual performance, there must be absolute trust and confidence between assessor and assessee.

Notes

1.   If the hourly rate is too low, no effective wage/work relationship is possible. Pay is a mark of value, and low pay in the eyes of the employees means low value. People take low paid jobs only because they have to and until something better comes along.

2.   Turnover, absenteeism and low productivity all rise where the employees are, or perceive themselves to be, unvalued or undervalued.

3.   Overpayment does not make mundane or boring work more interesting. It makes it more bearable (see section on motivation above). When pay rates rise, there is a short-term benefit. This is followed by employees reverting to previous levels of activity and approach.

4.   Those who work from a variety of locations, are normally provided with transport, travelling time and expenses and additional allowances. These are either paid separately or else worked into the total salary package.

5.   Those who work on a variety of jobs which change frequently or regularly, or whose hours and shift patterns change frequently and regularly are provided with additional payments to compensate. This is done either by:

   (a)   making a point of itemizing each of the elements included in the wage or salary. This satisfies the perceptions and expectations of employees. It requires additional administration and in large organizations, with highly complex work hours and shift patterns, this is a heavy additional cost;

   (b)   paying a relatively high single wage or salary in return for which the employee works as necessary and directed. This takes a greater level of introduction and understanding; the payback is to remove the administrative burden indicated above.

6.   Integrity and equality – any system of payment must be understood and valued. It should treat people equally and with respect.

        There is never a sound or honest reason for rewarding one group of the workforce at the expense of others. The effect is always to demoralize those who lose out. The longer-term effect is to enhance any divisions that already exist between the different

elements of the workforce as they jockey for position to ensure that they are not the ones to lose out in the future.

7.   By law, an itemized pay statement is required for all employees. This shows each element that makes up the gross pay, each deduction made before payment and the amount of net pay.

8.   Pay rises, bonuses and other rewards should always be paid on the date on which they are due. Again, it is a mark of respect and value.

9.   Economic rent is the payment of very high rates for particular forms of expertise. While this is clearly essential in some circumstances, it should be recognized that the appearance of overpayment of some individuals is likely to have a detrimental and damaging effect on the rest of the workforce. Payment of high salaries which distorts the general pattern should only be contemplated when all other approaches have failed.

10.   Payment of low rates is certainly possible for unskilled staff in periods of high unemployment (e.g. the UK in the mid-1990s). Again, this should only really be contemplated if there is no alternative – for example, if the organization is going through a lean time. Underpayment is a mark of contempt for the staff.

11.   Pay freezes and reductions are also demoralizing and damaging to the staff. Again, they should only be contemplated when there is no other alternative.

Benefits

Benefits are items and services offered by employers to employees as part of the reward package. They consist of the following.

- **General benefits:** loans (for example, for season tickets), pension arrangements (contributory and non-contributory), subsidies (on company products, canteen, travel), car, telephone/car phone, private health care, training and development, luncheon vouchers.

- **Flexible benefits:** packages that all staff members can have access to if they wish to do so and which are offered to all staff members on the same basis.

- **Chains of gold or super-benefits:** school holidays (teachers); cheap loans (banks, building societies), free/cheap travel

(railways, shipping, airlines), pension arrangements (for older and longer serving staff).

The main reasons for using benefits are as follows.

- To encourage certain types of behaviour – for example, paying for training courses; paying subscriptions to professional associations and expert bodies; paying for accommodation while employees are working away from home.

- To encourage potential employees to join the organization – for example, relocation expenses, travel packages, use of company cars.

- As a way of retaining employees – for example, the opportunity to buy shares; increases in holiday entitlements in line with length of service; enhanced pension rights.

- The recognition of long service – for example, presentations after specific time periods.

- As a demonstration of being a caring employer – for example, sick pay; occupational health schemes; life assurance; health insurance and private health care plans; school fee plans.

- A commitment to equal opportunities – for example, nurseries; career break schemes and sabbaticals; flexible hours and locations.

Flexible benefits may also be used as a means of recognizing and indicating enhanced status – for example, allowing certain grades of employee to travel first class, stay in 4 and 5-star accommodation, providing high quality cars. However, this invariably detracts from the fundamental basis of equality that is essential to all flexible working arrangements.

In general, therefore, benefit packages will be made available to staff on an even footing. The only exceptions are where the benefit is work-related to certain categories of employee; even in these circumstances, the offering of benefits to certain groups of employees but not others must be on operational grounds alone.

Notes

1. **Choosing the benefits**
   The mix of benefits available depends on the patterns of work of the employees and the nature of the organization's business.

Some organizations do have hook-ups with others – for example, working for a travel agent gives an entitlement to free travel with certain airlines and shipping and railway companies; some organizations provide discount cards for their staff to be used at department stores, supermarkets, travel agencies and finance companies.

Benefit choice is most effective when things that are offered benefit all employees, where the ability to choose is based on personal and occupational circumstances, and where the benefits are not seen as privileges only available to a chosen few.

2.   **Benefits and cash alternatives**
Some organizations allow their staff either to choose the benefit or to take a cash equivalent. For example, if it is not possible for an employee to use up their total annual leave allowance during the course of a year for operational reasons, then a cash alternative should always be made available. If it is not possible for a parent to bring their child into the company nursery, a cash payment should be made instead.

3.   **Individual choice**
Giving individuals the choice of determining which benefits they require from a total package enables them to weigh up their own current needs and how their organization can best serve them. This reinforces the positive message that the organization cares about them as an individual as well as an employee.

4.   **Chains of gold**
Chains of gold are extremely attractive to employees when they first come to work and as long as the relationship between employee and employer remains productive and positive. They become a burden on the individual when the relationship is lost. This is especially true where a financial commitment has been entered into as an integral part of the employment package – a free/cheap loan from a bank or building society; subscription to a pension or life assurance arrangement as part of a flexible benefits plan. There is at least a moral duty on employers to make arrangements for as painless an arrangement as possible to be entered into when the employee seeks to leave the organization. In this way, the employee concerned is looked after to the best of the organization's ability for the whole term of their employment. It also gives positive messages to those remaining in that they are reassured that, if they do suddenly need to leave, they will be taken care of properly.

Summary

Managing the flexible workforce is about creating the conditions necessary for high quality, productive, profitable and effective work to take place. This is only possible where a good environment is created and adequate equipment and technology is present.

In order to be able to maximize and optimize this, high quality staff have to be employed. A flexible work approach means that high quality staff are:

- positive and committed, highly trained, able to work in a range of different areas and able to use as much of their capability as is required;

- committed to continuous development and training and committed to the long-term future of the organization.

This in turn is only possible if there is top quality management and supervision. Top quality managers and supervisors are also highly trained and expert, highly committed and highly motivated. They also take an active responsibility for the long-term and continued success of the organizations for which they work.

At an operational level, effective management of the flexible workforce lies in the ability to make each of the different components work effectively in particular situations. It also means recognizing and meeting the obligations to the staff. Above all, it means keeping in mind that the purpose of flexible working – indeed of all working – is to create top quality products and services which customers wish to buy and use, and which will encourage them to keep coming back for more.

5 Summary and conclusion

Flexibility and flexible working comes from an attitude, a culture, a corporate state of mind. This is that much more can be achieved by people who are prepared, willing and able to do more than by people placed in straight-jacketed, formalized job descriptions outside which they never stray.

Flexible working requires the right conditions. Creating these is a matter of organizational policy and strategy. It requires long-term and continuous investment in premises, technology, the working environment and above all, the staff. The paybacks are in continuous profits, successes and effectiveness – measured especially over the longer term.

Flexible working requires a distinctive type of management and supervision. Managers and supervisors work close to the staff, as well as with the production targets, procedures and systems. To make this humanly possible, the procedures and systems are kept as simple as possible so that time and resources are released for primary purposes.

Managers and supervisors are highly trained and skilled. They have a set of priorities based on customer satisfaction and product/service quality. This in turn is only possible if high quality staff are engaged.

High quality staff are highly flexible, skilled and trained, highly motivated and committed, and as well paid as possible. They share in organizational profits and successes. They participate in development. They also participate in mistakes and failures which are put right from a positive point of view of learning and development.

High quality staff are ready, willing and able to do whatever is required in the organization's best interests. They must be highly motivated as well as highly skilled. This comes about as the result of:

- attention to the issues raised by engaging in different patterns of working;

- understanding the priorities and demands of staff of different types and levels of expertise;

- understanding the pressures brought about by different patterns of working and attendance;

- creating a basic set of values based on positivism and equality;

- engaging the high levels of work for high rewards equation;

- recognizing the relationship between expectation, effort and reward, and harmonizing these as far as possible;

- removing from the working environment those things that tend to demotivate, especially adversarial and distant managerial and supervisory styles, differentials based on status and elitism, and uncertainties in communications.

The onus is on the organization and its managers to get their part right. As long as this is done, they have the right to expect the staff to work in the ways directed. This is supported by a positive and effective style of management, simple procedures, effective job and work design, attention to selection and flexible contracts of employment. Potential levels of motivation in flexible working are very high and the conditions for these must be created by management.

The management of opportunities and activities is driven by creating conditions where problems are kept to a minimum. This comes about first and foremost by understanding the nature of the work demanded, the type of working environment and the opportunities and constraints presented. All of this indicates where problems are certain or likely to arise. Steps can then be taken to minimize their effects. Where this is not possible, compensations, variety, enhancement and enrichment have to be offered for best results. In the longer term, this indicates the need for work technology and environment redesign. In the shorter term, there is pressure on managers and supervisors to monitor the effectiveness of work and the working environment, to identify issues as they arise and to take whatever steps are necessary to minimize their effects.

The approach to problems when they do arise is to nip them in the bud. This is a key contribution of visible and positive styles of management and supervision. Speedy and effective responses to all staff matters is essential. This keeps problems of discipline, grievances and dismissals to a minimum. Poor or falling levels of performance and behaviour are picked up and rectified early. This is essential, especially for those who work away from the organization, and those whose hours are short or attendance infrequent. Putting people through disciplinary and grievance procedures is kept to a minimum and only used where all else has failed. It reduces administration and frees up resources for productive, effective – and profitable – activities. Where procedures are engaged they are operated as quickly as possible. Natural justice, fairness and reasonableness must be adhered to, but none of these are ever excuses for being dilatory or for institutionalizing problems.

Communications are simple and direct, and of high quality. The best approach again is the visible, underpinned by a fundamental soundness and integrity in the working relationship and by clear and unambiguous documentation, written in the language of the receiver.

Flexibility requires a fundamental shift of traditional organizational approaches, from the rigid and hierarchical to the pursuit of product and service quality and excellence. This is supported by high quality human relations, high levels of attention to product and service, and an understanding of what constitutes customer satisfaction. It enables a much greater opportunity for products and services to be offered to customers and more scope for business development. It enables sectors of society to have job and work opportunities where these would not otherwise exist. It enables organizations to have access to much greater pools of capability, expertise, talent and potential than would otherwise be possible.

Paradoxically, flexibility is conformist. It is based on high and distinctive standards of behaviour, attitude, performance and commitment. Those who work in flexible organizations accept these – or do not work. If they are to be effective and successful, they must be capable of harmonizing staff and organization, of finding and developing mutuality of interest in the working situation. In flexible working, there is no room for inflexibility or extensive procedural systems. There is no room either for cosy little jobs or long-term steady-state unchanging patterns of work or occupation.

Above all, it is an opportunity – for business to transform its activities and service quality; for public services to get to grips with often very limited resources; for managers to develop real management (as opposed to administrative and procedural) expertise; for customers to extend their range of choice and opportunity; and for staff – for people from all walks of life – to realize their potential, pursue their interests and lead varied, productive and rewarding working lives.

Glossary

ACAS The Advisory, Conciliation and Arbitration Service. ACAS provides advice and guidance on all matters of employment and may be called upon to intervene in disputes and problems. ACAS may be contacted at any time on any general employment matter.

BS 5750/ISO 9000 The Award of the British Standards Institute (BSI) for total quality management, and high levels of commitment to staff and customers.

Career break The practice of offering extended periods of leave to staff after a certain period of employment. This normally takes the form of a sabbatical (in which the employee is free to do whatever they choose during the career break), or time off for child care. Those who take career breaks are given full continuity of employment when they return to work.

Conformism The setting of distinctive patterns of attitudes and behaviour to which all employees are required to agree.

Contract of employment The formalization of the working relationship between employer and employee.

Contract for services The formalization of the working relationship between one organization and another, e.g. a subcontractor, an agency.

Core and peripheral workforce The core is the permanent workforce; the peripheral is made up of those parts of the workforce which are hired and employed at specific times or for particular purposes.

Corporate culture The combination of organizational activities, behaviour and attitudes – 'the way things are done'.

Counselling The practice of giving personal support to members of staff in difficulty, with problems, or on any general matter of employment.

Custom and practice The work patterns and activities which grow up as a matter of habit over a period of time.

Data Protection Act 1988 The law that governs what may be held on file about employees. Any information that is held about employees must be made available to them (this includes both paper and electronic files).

Discrimination Practice of differentiating between people on particular grounds. Discrimination may be lawful – differentiating on grounds of capability or attitude; or unlawful – discriminating on grounds of race, gender, marital status, membership/not of a trade union, etc.

Employment Department The Employment Department of the Department for Education and Employment issues guidelines and advice to employers on all aspects of working.

Employment protection The legal protection from bullying, victimization, harassment or discrimination at all times, and protection from unfair dismissal – i.e. dismissal for no good reason, or when procedures have not been followed – for all employees after two years' service.

Employment Protection Consolidation Act 1987 (EPCA) The main law that governs the contract of employment and other aspects of the working relationship.

Empowerment The practice of giving individual employees responsibility, autonomy and authority over the nature and quality of their work.

Equality The principle on which all employees are treated.

Flexible benefits Rewards and advantages gained by employees as the result of working for the particular organization, and to which they may subscribe if they so choose.

Full-time and part-time working The description of the traditional work pattern of the UK; as the result of flexible working and changes in employment legislation, the distinction has become blurred. For best practice and best results, full-time and part-time employees are treated the same.

Genuine occupational qualification (GOQ) Any skill or quality required of an individual to do a particular job. A GOQ is the only reason why any form of race, gender or disability discrimination may occur.

Health and Safety at Work Act 1974 (HASAWA) The legislation governing all matters of health and safety at work in the UK.

Homeworking The practice of having people working from their homes rather than from organizational premises.

Implied terms Those matters not stated in a contract of employment but which may reasonably be expected to apply.

Incentive schemes The practice of offering additional rewards for successful and effective work.

Induction The practice of settling people into their place of work; the practice of instilling the required standards, attitudes and behaviour at the outset of employment.

Investors In People (IIP) An award made by government to employers confirming the employer's commitment to its workforce.

Job description A statement of tasks and activities to be carried out by the job holder.

Job enrichment The practice of extending and enlarging the quality and volume of work to be carried out by an individual.

Job share The practice of dividing up a full-time job between two or three employees (job sharers).

Just in time The ability to call up staff, supplies, components and equipment at short notice whenever they are required.

Labour costs The total cost of employing people. Labour costs always include salary, national insurance, pension, equipment, accommodation, heating and lighting; some employers also include supervision, training, down/unproductive time, other benefits and rewards. It is usual to regard labour costs as fixed costs (rather than variable costs).

Labour/employee/industrial relations The regulation of activities, behaviour and attitudes that exist at places of work; systems and procedures for the resolution of conflict; the behavioural aspects of staff management.

Managing by walking about (MBWA) A term used to describe highly visible and personal styles of supervision.

Maternity rights The legal requirement to give all female employees 14 weeks' maternity leave regardless of length of service or hours worked; the legal requirement to give female employees up to 29 weeks' maternity leave after two years' continuous service; the requirement to give all pregnant female employees reasonable time off to attend pre-natal health checks and care.

Organization development (OD) Organizational commitment to continuous improvement in all areas; commitment to continuous staff training; commitment to job and work enlargement; commitment to streamlining and simplification of procedures.

Person specification The statement of qualities and attributes required of a person to do a particular job. This normally mirrors the job description.

Premium rates/economic rent The need to make high levels of pay and reward for certain types of work; the ability to demand high rates of pay and reward for certain types of work.

Quality of working life The creation of effective and successful work environments, in which high and successful levels of output can be achieved.

Recognition The relationship between employers and their trade unions; all employers have the right to recognize or not to recognize trade unions.

Rostering The practice of organizing staff into distinctive work patterns.

Seven-point plan A form of person specification.

Shift patterns The organization of people into regular times of work. Term-time working, the practice of employing people to work during school term-times and requiring them to take substantial periods of leave during the school holidays. Continuity of employment is normally guaranteed.

Telecommuting The practice of 'commuting', locking into working systems, maintaining a working relationship between employer and employee, through the use of electronic supervision systems, e-mail and other information technology.

Teleconferencing The practice of holding meetings and conferences through the telephone network, supported by someone at the centre of the meeting having a multi-audio facility.

Testing for employability The practice of requiring potential employees to take tests that indicate their ability, aptitude, potential or attitude for and towards particular types of work.

Total quality management (TQM) An approach to organization management based on product, service and working life quality.

Trade union A national institution whose objectives are to represent the best interests of their members in places of work.

Trade Union Reform and Employment Rights Act 1993 (TURERA) The employment legislation that guarantees minimum maternity rights, and employment protection to all members of staff regardless of whether they are full-time or part-time.

Transfer of Undertakings Protection of Employment (TUPE) Regulations (1981) The regulations that guarantee continuity of employment and protection of terms and conditions of employment (including pay) at the time when ownership of an organization or function is changed.